YOUNG ROBIN HOOD

Jon Klein

BROADWAY PLAY PUBLISHING INC
224 E 62nd St, NY, NY 10065
www.broadwayplaypub.com
info@broadwayplaypub.com

First printing: June 2015
I S B N: 978-0-88145-634-9

Book design: Marie Donovan
Page make-up: Adobe Indesign
Typeface: Palatino
Printed and bound in the U S A

YOUNG ROBIN HOOD was first produced by Round House Theatre in Bethesda, Maryland; the first performance was on 28 November 2012. The cast and creative contributors were:

DIANA/SPIRIT	Emma Crane Jaster
PHILIP	Davis Chandler Hasty
ROBIN HOOD	Joe Isenberg
WILLIAM FITZOOTH	Craig Wallace
GUY OF GISBOURNE	JJ Kaczynski
MARIAN	Laura C Harris
SHERIFF OF NOTTINGHAM	Mitchell Hébert
MUCH	Sean Silvia
JOAN	Allie Villarreal
ROSALIND	Kimberly Schraf
AN ABBOTT/RICHARD	Jeff Allin
Director	Derek Goldman
Scenic designer	Misha Kachman
Costume designer	Ivania Stack
Lighting designer	Kenton Yeager
Composer/sound designer	Matthew M Nielson
Props designer	Andrea Moore
Fight choreographer	Casey Kaleba
Movement coach	Emma Jaster
Stage manager	Maribeth Chaprnka

CHARACTERS & SETTING

Spoken roles: 7 males, 4 females:

ROBIN, *a lad of sixteen*

WILLIAM FITZOOTH, *his adoptive father, one of the King's Foresters*

PHILIP, ROBIN's *schoolmate*

GUY OF GISBOURNE, PHILIP's *father, a wealthy landowner of Nottinghamshire; also* CELLKEEPER, EXECUTIONER

AN ABBOT, *(in disguise)*

MARIAN, *a young lady, about* ROBIN's *age*

ROSALIND, *a widow*

MUCH, *her son, a boy*

JOAN, *her daughter, a bit older*

SHERIFF OF NOTTINGHAM, MARIAN's *father*

DIANA, *a falcon (and possibly other creatures—stag, bear, etc)*

Locations:

In and around Sherwood Forest, England, and occasionally in the nearby village of Nottingham.

PRODUCTION NOTES

The different locales may be suggested by light and sound, rather than physical elements. The premiere production at Roundhouse Theatre used a unit set, which suggested Sherwood Forest, and a number of ramps, levels and bridges that suggested a playground.

Also in that production, the character of DIANA *(the falcon) was played by a performer who also portrayed the other animals mentioned in the script (and a few more of her own design), as well as embodying the natural elements of the forest. For that reason, she was referred to in the program as* DIANA *and the* SPIRIT OF THE FOREST. *Such use of future performers is up to subsequent directors.*

The fight sequences may be choreographed more elaborately than indicated here in simple descriptions. For example, the Roundhouse production included a fight between JOAN *and* ROBIN *that took place underwater.*

A note about arrows. Real arrows (with dulled points) were handled in the Roundhouse production, but never actually shot. Casey Kaleba, the fight choreographer, taugh the actors how to draw their bows but to hold their arrows to the side *of the bowstring, so no arrows could be accidentally released. The arrows were lowered with the bows as soon as the bowstrings were released—all covered with realistic sound effects. This stage magic gave the* illusion *of arrows being fired, and is recommended.*

PLAYWRIGHT'S NOTE:

Any version of the Robin Hood myth relies on equal parts familiarity and speculation. To this day, scholars cannot agree on whether Robin Hood even existed, much less where and when. Our modern notions of this ancient story have evolved more from Hollywood treatments than the original ballad sources.

But that's not necessarily inappropriate, since the very first findings of Robin Hood tales—in the early sixteenth century—indicate a story that already was exaggerated and romanticized out of proportion. And although there are previous documentations of men arrested under the name "Robynhode," they seem to suggest that the name was already a pseudonym for certain outlaws who had popular appeal—especially in the context of cruel and corrupt governments.

So I've borrowed a few elements from the traditional tales, made others up entirely, and mixed them all up out of their usual order. In the example of Marian, she was added on much later to the tales, and is a product of sheer imagination. So I've taken some liberties with her traditional role as Robin's loyal but passive girlfriend. And as for "Little John", well, you'll see.

ACT ONE

Scene One

(Lights up on the magical mystery of Sherwood Forest, with beams of sunlight slicing through the mighty oaks.)

(The exterior of a modest, well-tended cottage is suggested, as well as a particularly large oak tree.)

(PHILIP enters at a run, searching for someone. His clothes are practical, though well-tailored.)

PHILIP: Where are you? Show yourself! *(He unsuccessfully searches some hiding places.)* What are you, afraid? If you want a fight, then face me man to man!

ROBIN: *(Offstage)* Here I am! *(He swings onstage from a rope.)* But where is this man you speak of?

PHILIP: You see him before you. But all I see is a boy. Or are you a forest sprite?

ROBIN: Be careful, friend. Or I may take offense.

PHILIP: Oh, really? And what do sprites do when challenged? Fly away?

ROBIN: Enough talk. If it's a fight you want—then you'll get one.

(ROBIN grabs two long broadstaves that lean against the house, and throws one to PHILIP.)

PHILIP: All right. Let's see what you're made of.

ROBIN: You'll find I'm harder to fell than one of Sherwood's mighty oaks.

PHILIP: If you're made of wood, I'm made of stone.

ROBIN: Your head, perhaps. But don't worry, I won't be aiming that high.

(ROBIN *approaches* PHILIP *and swings his broadstaff.* PHILIP *jumps back. An elaborate—and ultimately harmless—fight ensues, more for the fun of maneuvering escapes than to land actual blows. Both boys have a great time, whooping it up and exulting in their own "bravery.")*

(Eventually, ROBIN*'s father,* WILLIAM*, comes out of the cottage.* ROBIN*'s back is to him, but* PHILIP *freezes when he sees* WILLIAM *approach.)*

PHILIP: Robin—stop!

ROBIN: Ah! The great warrior is frozen with fear! Time to strike the finishing blow!

(ROBIN *raises his broadstaff high, but* WILLIAM *simply takes it away from him, from behind.)*

ROBIN: Hey! *(He turns to face his father.)* Oh. Hello, Father.

WILLIAM: Good afternoon, Robin.

ROBIN: We were just…um…

WILLIAM: How many times have I told you boys? A broadstaff is not to be used as a weapon. It's for defense only. To keep your balance, in case you're attacked by an enemy.

PHILIP: He started it.

ROBIN: I didn't hear any complaints from you.

WILLIAM: This thing is not for fighting. It's to <u>keep</u> from fighting. Which should always be your first choice.

ROBIN: Oh, Father. Only a coward would choose not to fight.

WILLIAM: Wrong. A coward backs *away* from a fight.

PHILIP: What's the difference?

WILLIAM: You must always stand your ground.

(PHILIP *and* ROBIN *stare at* WILLIAM *blankly.*)

WILLIAM: I'll show you. Robin, grab that tree branch. Philip, use your staff. Now I'll stand here like this… (*He takes a wide stance, and holds the broadstaff in front of him horizontally.*) Now the two of you rush me, and strike each end of my staff with your own sticks. Hit it as hard as you can. I guarantee that I will not budge an inch.

ROBIN: Impossible.

WILLIAM: Try it.

(PHILIP *and* ROBIN *walk some distance from* WILLIAM, *then turn.*)

WILLIAM: Now go. Run!

(PHILIP *and* ROBIN *take off running together as fast as they can, their sticks held high to smash against* WILLIAM's *broadstaff. But as soon as they reach him,* WILLIAM *drops his staff to the ground, causing the boys to swing their sticks against empty air. They both tumble to the ground, bruised and out of breath.*)

(WILLIAM *turns and looks down at them.*)

WILLIAM: That's how you stand your ground.

ROBIN: You cheated!

WILLIAM: No, son. I simply chose not to fight. And I won.

(WILLIAM *heads back to the house, taking the two broadstaffs with him, and leaving the boys on the ground.*)

PHILIP: Your father is a lunatic.

ROBIN: I know.

(Suddenly, a large commotion is heard in the forest, with branches breaking and leaves rustling. A stag enters the area to the side of the house. It draws everyone's attention, and keeps WILLIAM from entering the house.)

PHILIP: Look! A stag!

(They run to the upstage side of the house, and look behind.)

ROBIN: It jumped the fence! I'll get my bow!

WILLIAM: No, son.

ROBIN: Why not?

WILLIAM: It's become forbidden.

ROBIN: To hunt game on our own property?

PHILIP: Your father's right.

WILLIAM: Prince John has rewritten the Forest Laws, in King Richard's absence. Now all deer and wild boar are reserved for members of the Royal Family. No exceptions.

ROBIN: But they only hunt out of boredom! They don't even need the meat to feed themselves!

WILLIAM: Neither do we. We have enough rabbit and squirrel meat to last the summer.

ROBIN: Squirrel? I'd rather eat tree bark!

PHILIP: Why does it just stand there? Why doesn't it run away?

WILLIAM: It has instincts. It knows it's safe near the King's Forester.

(GUY [pronounced "Gee", with a hard G] OF GISBOURNE enters, a dandy in impractical attire. He awkwardly carries a large hunting bow.)

GUY: Which way did it go?

PHILIP: Father! What are you doing here?

GUY: Hunting, of course. Who are these people? This boy looks familiar.

PHILIP: He's been to our house, Father. We attend school together. This is Robin Fitzooth. And his father. They live here.

GUY: Then they should have seen where that stag went. I've been chasing him all day.

ROBIN: He's in the back of our house. Just standing there.

(GUY *goes to the corner of the cottage and looks.*)

GUY: Excellent! Now if everyone would please be still, this should make for an easy trophy.

(GUY *raises the bow, but* WILLIAM *grabs it out of his hands.*)

GUY: What is the meaning of this, sir?

WILLIAM: Very simple, my lord. I am the King's Forester, and my job is to protect the wildlife and vegetation of Sherwood Forest.

GUY: I have every right to hunt game here! I have permission from Prince John himself!

WILLIAM: Fine. Then simply show me your permit, and you may continue your hunt. May I see it, please?

GUY: I don't have anything in writing.

WILLIAM: I'm very sorry, my lord. The laws are very precise. No hunting without the Prince's written permission.

GUY: You are to make an exception for me! I'm of noble birth!

WILLIAM: Which is why you have no need of deer meat. You can buy all you want at the market.

GUY: How dare you!

PHILIP: Umm , father…

GUY: Not now, Philip. I'm trying to talk some sense into this *peasant* before the deer gets away.

PHILIP: That's what I'm trying to tell you—it's gone.

GUY: What? *(He looks again, and stamps his foot in anger.)*

WILLIAM: You may have this back now.

GUY: Blast! No telling which way it went. *(He turns back to* WILLIAM.*)* I hope you're satisfied. You may be sure the Sheriff will be hearing about this.

WILLIAM: You can tell him that I was simply enforcing the law. Just as he does.

GUY: He has his own way of interpreting the law. As I'm sure you *know*. *(He turns to* PHILIP.*)* Come, Philip. Let's away from these unpleasantly common folk.

ROBIN: *(To* PHILIP*)* Come back tomorrow. We'll continue our training.

GUY: I can assure you that Philip will not be returning tomorrow or any other time. His association with the likes of you will be limited to his schooling. Where apparently, they are teaching him how to let ANIMALS ESCAPE!

*(*GUY *walks off in a fury.* PHILIP *whispers to* ROBIN.*)*

PHILIP: Just give him a day or two. This will all be forgotten.

*(*PHILIP *follows* GUY *offstage.* ROBIN *and* WILLIAM *watch them go.)*

ROBIN: What a windbag.

WILLIAM: Robin! That's enough!

ROBIN: What's the matter, Father?

WILLIAM: You are such a naïve boy. You have no idea of how things work around here. Guy of Gisbourne is the largest landowner in Nottinghamshire. Of course the Sheriff is going to listen to him. It's in his *interest.*

ROBIN: But as you said—you were only enforcing the law.

WILLIAM: Laws can be ignored—if they cause too much trouble. And I may have just caused too much trouble for Sir Guy.

ROBIN: What will happen?

(WILLIAM *realizes he's worrying* ROBIN. *He puts his hand on his shoulder and smiles.*)

WILLIAM: Nothing, I'm sure. No major harm done. Just some wounded pride—and a trampled garden. You better see what kind of damage that stag did behind the house.

(WILLIAM *goes back in the house, leaving* ROBIN *alone. He starts off towards the garden, watches the door of the cottage, and stretches out on the ground to nap.* WILLIAM *comes back out, and sees* ROBIN *slacking off. He shakes his head with a disapproving smile, and goes to the back of the house himself.*)

(*Lights shift.*)

Scene Two

(*Time has passed, and the sunlight intensifies.* ROBIN *remains asleep on the ground.*)

(*Suddenly, a dead bird drops from the sky above, landing near* ROBIN, *waking him. He picks it up and curiously scans the skies.* MARIAN *enters and addresses him. She wears a fine riding outfit, suitable for a young lady of means and style.* MARIAN *also wears a leather glove, upon which is perched a large falcon,* DIANA.)

MARIAN: Thank you, boy. For retrieving my pigeon. You may hand it over now.

ROBIN: *Your* pigeon?

MARIAN: Yes, my falcon has killed it. So it belongs to me.

ROBIN: I would not be so quick to admit it. Hunting is forbidden in Sherwood Forest.

MARIAN: Oh, yes, those absurd Forest Laws of Prince John. I can assure you they don't apply to me. So stop being such a silly boy and hand over my bird.

ROBIN: Are you a member of the Royal Family?

MARIAN: Certainly not.

ROBIN: Then you and your falcon have broken the law.

MARIAN: Do you intend to have us both arrested?

ROBIN: Just you. Not the falcon. It's just a stupid bird and doesn't understand the law. But you should know better.

MARIAN: She's not an it. And I'm willing to bet she's smarter than you. Her name is Diana. I named her after—

ROBIN: The goddess of hunting. And protector of the Sacred Woods. I've studied Roman mythology too.

MARIAN: You know how to read?

ROBIN: My father taught me.

MARIAN: Well then. You're not as dumb as you look.

ROBIN: I am so. I mean, I am not. I mean…umm…

MARIAN: I take it back.

(The falcon seems to get agitated, perhaps laughing at ROBIN.*)*

MARIAN: I know, dear, this silly boy is very droll. But let's not get too excited.

(MARIAN *puts a hood over the falcon's head, to calm her down.* DIANA *submits without a fight.* MARIAN *perches her nearby.*)

ROBIN: Is that necessary?

MARIAN: The hood keeps her calm. Her claws are razor sharp, you know. I can even feel them through this glove. But she'll obey me.

ROBIN: That's amazing. How did you train her?

MARIAN: The same way you train any simple creature. With trust and affection. And a little bit of food. (*She produces a pear from her pocket.*) Would you like a pear?

ROBIN: Yes, please.

MARIAN: Then bring me that pigeon, would you?

(ROBIN *automatically picks up the bird and approaches* MARIAN—*then suddenly stops.*)

ROBIN: Very funny.

MARIAN: Funny or not, I insist you hand it over. Or you may face certain consequences.

ROBIN: What now, a threat?

(MARIAN *removes the hood from* DIANA.)

MARIAN: Diana—fetch his cap!

(DIANA *flies across and grabs* ROBIN'*s hat, frightening him.*)

ROBIN: Hey! Stop it!

MARIAN: Bring it to me!

(DIANA *flies back to* MARIAN'*s glove.*)

MARIAN: Good girl!

ROBIN: Very impressive.

MARIAN: I'm glad you think so.

ROBIN: Now what must I do to get it back?

MARIAN: Just ask.

ROBIN: May I have my cap?

MARIAN: Not me. Ask *Diana.*

ROBIN: What? I'm not going to talk to a stupid bird.

MARIAN: I believe we've already established the relative intelligence of my falcon. Now she requires an apology as well.

ROBIN: No.

MARIAN: Do you want your hat back or not?

ROBIN: Not that much.

MARIAN: Have it your way. But I will have my pigeon.

ROBIN: It isn't yours. The birds of Sherwood Forest are protected against trespassers. Even lowly pigeons.

(WILLIAM *appears from around the house, drawn by the sound of the argument.)*

MARIAN: How dare you? Do you know who you're speaking to, you filthy boy?

(WILLIAM *inserts himself between them.)*

WILLIAM: Probably not. But I do.

ROBIN: Father—this girl claims she has some special permission to hunt in the forest.

WILLIAM: It's all right, Robin. Let her go.

MARIAN: There, you see?

ROBIN: What makes her so special? Who is she?

WILLIAM: Robin—allow me to introduce you to Marian. Daughter to the Sheriff of Nottingham.

ROBIN: The Sheriff's daughter?

WILLIAM: That's right. *(He turns to* MARIAN.*)* I'm William Fitzooth, chief forester of Sherwood. And this is my son, Robin.

ACT ONE   11

MARIAN: I suggest you teach your son a few courtly
manners. Otherwise he should keep his brutish
behavior confined to the bears and squirrels. He
wouldn't last a day in real society.

ROBIN: What kind of society is left, after your father
taxes the people to oblivion?

(WILLIAM *gestures to* ROBIN *to be quiet.*)

WILLIAM: I'll talk to the boy. And you may have your
bird now.

(WILLIAM *takes the pigeon from* ROBIN, *and hands it to*
MARIAN.)

MARIAN: Thank you. I will mention your kindness
to my father. Speaking of which—Master Fitzooth.
My father requests your company at dinner in his
castle tomorrow evening at eight. Will you accept his
invitation?

WILLIAM: Of course. Is there any particular...reason...
for this offer?

MARIAN: None that I am aware of. Though I believe
Sir Guy will also be there. And his son, whom I
understand is a well-mannered and chivalrous young
man.

WILLIAM: Philip.

MARIAN: Just so. Philip. I look forward to meeting him.
It will be an excellent change of pace from the other
boys I meet around here. (*She turns back to* ROBIN.)
By the way. My father said you are invited as well. If
you can tear yourself away from your precious forest,
doing whatever you do to entertain yourself here,
collecting pine cones or playing with squirrels.

ROBIN: I'll tell you what I think of your invitation—

(WILLIAM *gives* ROBIN *a small smack in the head.*)

WILLIAM: He accepts.

(ROBIN *gives* WILLIAM *a steely look.*)

MARIAN: Good. Perhaps your son will even comb his hair for the occasion. In the meantime, we should probably hide it, so as not to scare small children. Diana!

(DIANA *flies to* ROBIN *and drops the hat.*)

ROBIN: I still refuse to apologize.

MARIAN: I am keenly aware of that. Perhaps you don't have the vocabulary. No matter—I suppose even a backwoods boy like you can learn a manner or two. With the proper...training. I will tell Father to expect both of you tomorrow night.

WILLIAM: Much obliged.

MARIAN: Come, Diana. Let's show your prize to Daddy.

(DIANA *and* MARIAN *exit.*)

WILLIAM: Are you mad? Do you want to throw us both in jail? Her father has hung people for less insolence than you just showed. And to his own daughter!

ROBIN: So what? She's not royalty! The law says—

WILLIAM: The law is whatever the Sheriff decides it is!

(WILLIAM *calms down, and sits* ROBIN *down beside him on fallen tree trunk.*)

WILLIAM: Robin. Do you remember the story—about how I found you?

ROBIN: Yes, father.

WILLIAM: Right there— (*He points to the front porch of his house.*) —on my own steps. A newborn babe, less than a week old, laying in a straw basket too worn to be of any real use. Some poor woman knew that she could not care for her baby—whether from ill health or poverty we'll never know. But she came to me as someone who was known to protect the creatures of the forest. I swore on that day that unknown woman's trust in me would be justified. I would always keep you safe from harm, and teach you how to protect yourself.

ROBIN: I know, father.

WILLIAM: But when I turn around to find you endangering yourself, with your rash, unthinking temper...ah well, perhaps I ask too much.

ROBIN: But it doesn't seem fair that some people get to use the forest, only because they were born rich. While the poor people who need to hunt—just to feed themselves and their families—

WILLIAM: —are arrested for doing so. I know it's unfair. I don't always like it. But it's my job. A job which keeps you safe and puts food on your plate. And allows you to play about in the most beautiful forest on God's green earth. So please—just try not to get us both in trouble. Or killed. All right?

ROBIN: Are we in trouble, Father?

WILLIAM: I'm not sure. But I don't believe that girl has the guile to lead us into a trap. Besides, I think she likes you.

ROBIN: What? Didn't you see the way she treated me?

WILLIAM: Yes, I did. And I saw the way you treated her.

ROBIN: Yes! With contempt! And disgust!

WILLIAM: Uh-huh.

(ROBIN and WILLIAM go into the house.)

(Lights shift.)

Scene Three

*(Lights up on an area representing the courtyard of
Nottingham Castle, as the* SHERIFF *enters, followed by* GUY,
MARIAN, PHILIP, ROBIN *and* WILLIAM. *The courtyard is
lit by torches. The* SHERIFF *is armed with a large sword,
sheathed at his waist.)*

SHERIFF: I trust everyone enjoyed the pheasant.

GUY: Most excellent, your honor—prepared in the
Norman fashion, I believe.

SHERIFF: I don't cook it. I just kill it.

GUY: Ah. My mistake.

SHERIFF: The meat was a bit greasy, I thought. The
disadvantage of wild game.

ROBIN: From Sherwood Forest, no doubt.

SHERIFF: Ah—just like your father. Always the vigilant
one. Yes, I bagged that bird myself, not far from your
house.

ROBIN: I suppose as the Sheriff, the King's prohibitions
don't apply to you, either.

WILLIAM: Robin! Don't be impertinent.

SHERIFF: It's all right, Fitzooth. The boy is simply
curious. I'm always glad to see lads taking interest in
matters of the law. As a matter of fact, I invited you all
here on to discuss a certain matter pertaining to local
law enforcement.

WILLIAM: If this is about Sir Guy's complaint against
me—

GUY: I have a legitimate grievance, and you know it.
No mere forester can tell a nobleman what to do.

SHERIFF: He certainly can, by rule of the Prince.

WILLIAM: In point of fact, I was appointed by King Richard Lionheart.

ROBIN: Before his Highness abandoned England for a Crusade in foreign lands.

SHERIFF: I can assure you his brother John rules England with equal affection for his subjects.

ROBIN: Such as taxing the poor?

WILLIAM: Robin!

SHERIFF: Such a brave lad. I find such courage of convictions quite...amusing—in a boy his age.

WILLIAM: Forgive the boy, your honor. He knows nothing of politics.

SHERIFF: Don't fret, Fitzooth. My daughter tells me of your courtesy to her.

MARIAN: And to Diana.

ROBIN: Stupid bird.

SHERIFF: And I have brought Sir Guy here to offer his sincere apologies.

GUY: What? Apologize?

PHILIP: Your honor. With all due respect—my father does not deserve such humiliation.

GUY: Especially after the treatment I received from this...caretaker.

SHERIFF: In the eyes of the law, your treatment is quite lenient. I suggest you take my offer as an alternative to...harsher consequences.

GUY: I'm...very sorry.

SHERIFF: Now that was very good. The law is satisfied. Naturally, I'll issue a written permit to Sir Guy so that he may have full reign in Sherwood.

ROBIN: What? I thought only the Prince himself had that authority.

SHERIFF: I speak for the Prince in Nottinghamshire. Do not doubt that—boy.

WILLIAM: As I said, the boy knows less than nothing of legal matters. It will be my honor to welcome Sir Guy to the forest.

SHERIFF: Excellent. And don't worry about young Robin's behavior. As a matter of fact, I bring him here—and Philip too—to inform you about a vacancy in my men-at-arms. One of my lead archers had a little too much cider, and suffered an unfortunate accident with his own crossbow.

(They look at him quizzically.)

MARIAN: He was holding it backwards.

SHERIFF: And so I need someone who's good with a bow. My sources tell me your two boys are the best young archers in Nottinghamshire. I may have a job for one of you.

ROBIN: No thank you. I plan to help my father with his duties in the forest.

GUY: And my son has better things to do than stop poachers and petty thieves. He will have his hands full with the estate.

PHILIP: But that's so boring. To be one of the Sheriff's men! That's the life for me! Adventure and excitement!

ROBIN: And keeping the peasants in their place.

PHILIP: If need be.

SHERIFF: Well, this seems to be an easy choice.

WILLIAM: Wait a minute. A word with my son. If you please.

(The SHERIFF nods.)

(WILLIAM *takes* ROBIN *aside.*)

WILLIAM: Son, you will never get an opportunity like this again. I have no money to educate you properly, and you will not inherit anything from me but a broken down old cottage in the woods. This is steady work, with considerable prestige. And you will be under the protection of Prince John.

ROBIN: I don't need a Prince's protection.

WILLIAM: You *do*. Until Richard Lionheart returns from the foreign wars, and takes back his rightful place on the throne—we *all* need protection. I beg you to reconsider.

(*Pause.* ROBIN *looks away.*)

WILLIAM: Please, Robin. Do it for me.

(ROBIN looks at his father, and relents.

ROBIN: You've given me everything in this life. I don't see how I can deny you this wish.

(WILLIAM *hugs* ROBIN.)

(ROBIN *turns back to the* SHERIFF.)

ROBIN: Your honor—I have changed my mind.

PHILIP: No fair! I said yes first!

SHERIFF: Now, boys. Let's slow down. You're both young, and there's a long training session to enter my posse. But more importantly, I need some proof of these highly reported archery skills. So I propose a contest to decide which one will enter my force.

MARIAN: A competition! What fun!

SHERIFF: As you see, I've already set up the targets.

(MARIAN *hands the bows and arrows to the boys.*)

GUY: Son—I had great plans for you. Please don't throw them all away to be a common…policeman.

SHERIFF: Sir, I warn you—do not interfere. This boy—
how old are you?

PHILIP: Seventeen, Your honor. A year older than
Robin.

SHERIFF: Good. Then you're old enough to make his
own decisions, and not be coddled by dandies.

GUY: Who are you—what?

SHERIFF: Here lads. Take your arrows. Thirty paces
from the targets, if you both please. Marian—can you
see the targets well in this torchlight?

(MARIAN *moves to the side of the targets.*)

MARIAN: Yes, father.

SHERIFF: Good—you judge the shooting. One round of
five arrows each. You may start...now.

(PHILIP *and* ROBIN *both shoot their arrows at the targets,
alternating turns.*)

SHERIFF: Marian? Your judgment, if you please.

(MARIAN *examines* PHILIP's *target.*)

MARIAN: Philip's target. Two in the center...three in
the second ring.

GUY: I had...no idea!

(MARIAN *moves to* ROBIN's *target.*)

MARIAN: Robin's target...the same!

WILLIAM: That's the way, my boy!

SHERIFF: Interesting. In that case, I propose a final
competition I like to call "sudden death." One arrow
each. The closest to the center wins the match.

(MARIAN *takes two additional arrows, as* PHILIP *runs
toward her with apparent chivalry.*)

PHILIP: Allow me, Miss. Don't pierce your pretty hands
on those sharp points.

ROBIN: Don't worry about her. Hands that can withstand a falcon's claws have nothing to fear from arrowheads.

(PHILIP *slightly bends* ROBIN'*s arrow, without anyone seeming to notice. No one, that is, except for* MARIAN—*who catches him in the act.*)

(PHILIP *brings the arrow to* ROBIN.)

PHILIP: Don't be jealous, Rob. Not everyone can hold the same attraction to fine young ladies. It's a matter of breeding. And maturity.

ROBIN: What, her? I could care less. *(He grabs his arrow from* PHILIP.) And you're no better than me—in birth *or* target shooting.

PHILIP: We'll see.

(PHILIP *and* ROBIN *shoot again, with* PHILIP'*s arrow again hitting his target. But this time* ROBIN'*s arrow goes wild.*)

SHERIFF: I see the forester's son can't handle the pressure. Too bad.

MARIAN: Wait a minute.

(Everyone turns to MARIAN. *She points to* PHILIP.)

MARIAN: This one cheated.

GUY: What? That's an outrageous accusation!

MARIAN: Philip bent Robin's arrow when he took it from me. I saw him do it.

GUY: Philip would never cheat.

SHERIFF: My daughter has a keen sense of fairness. If she says something's wrong, I believe her.

(They all turn to PHILIP.)

ROBIN: I thought we were friends.

PHILIP: We are. But I need this, Robin! You can live as free as you like in Sherwood Forest. But I'm being groomed for a life like *his*.

GUY: Philip!

PHILIP: *(To* ROBIN*)* Surely you understand.

ROBIN: You still didn't have to cheat.

MARIAN: You have to disqualify him, father.

SHERIFF: What for? I'm not hiring Philip for his honesty. Just his skills. Which seem exceptional.

MARIAN: Father! That's not fair!

SHERIFF: I decide what's fair.

WILLIAM: As you wish, your honor. We'll take our leave now.

SHERIFF: Not so fast, Fitzooth. As I said, I decide what's fair. And I'm interested in archery skill. Nothing more, nothing less. I won't disqualify the other boy. But I will give your son one last chance to prove he's better. So I will allow Robin one more arrow. *(He grabs an arrow himself.)*

PHILIP: You can't!

SHERIFF: Are you questioning my judgement, son?

*(*PHILIP *looks down, chagrined.)*

SHERIFF: I thought not. *(He turns to* ROBIN.*)* Now take that arrow, and shoot it.

(The SHERIFF *thrusts it at* ROBIN. ROBIN *hesitates.)*

SHERIFF: I said, take it!

*(*ROBIN *takes the arrow, looks at it, and throws it on the ground.)*

ROBIN: I'm not interested. *(He looks at* WILLIAM.*)* Sorry, father.

(The SHERIFF *puts his hand on his sword.* ROBIN *doesn't move.)*

ROBIN: Go ahead, Sheriff. I'm standing my ground.

*(*WILLIAM *moves behind his son, putting his hands on his shoulder.)*

WILLIAM: And I stand with him.

(The SHERIFF *hesitates. He turns and calmly holds out his hand to* PHILIP, *who is stunned and delighted.)*

SHERIFF: Welcome to the Sheriff's Guard, Philip of Gisbourne. Come—I will introduce you to your new master-in-training. *(He turns to* GUY.) Come sir, and we will discuss the payment arrangements.

GUY: Payment? Oh yes, of course. How much do I get for my son's services?

SHERIFF: You don't understand. You pay *me.* For the boy's training. Then—if he does well—he'll receive a fair salary.

PHILIP: Don't cause trouble, Father. Just pay him.

GUY: Hmmph.

(The SHERIFF *turns to* ROBIN *and* WILLIAM.)

SHERIFF: Fitzooth. You are the King's Forester, so I can't touch you or your son. Not yet. But I predict one of these days, you'll choose to defy the law—and that means you'll defy *me.* Come, gentlemen, let's draw up the contract.

(The SHERIFF *leaves with* GUY *and* PHILIP, *who turns back to* ROBIN.)

PHILIP: No hard feelings, I hope, Rob. It's better this way—for both of us. *(He follows the others.)*

*(*ROBIN *picks up the arrow he threw on the ground. He quickly paces to his previous spot, and rapidly "shoots" it.* MARIAN *examines the target.)*

MARIAN: Bullseye. You beat him.

WILLIAM: He already beat him—without the arrow.

ROBIN: Are you angry with me, Father?

WILLIAM: I have never been so proud of you, son. *(He turns to* MARIAN.) Thank you for your help, Marian. I hope we see you again.

MARIAN: I hope so too.

WILLIAM: Back to the forest for me. To pray for the return of Richard Lionheart. *(He exits.)*

*(*MARIAN *turns to the sulking* ROBIN.)*

MARIAN: I'm sorry.

ROBIN: You should be.

MARIAN: What do you mean? Your father said I helped you.

ROBIN: That's his opinion. Not mine.

MARIAN: What's wrong?

ROBIN: You had to say something, didn't you? I knew Philip bent that arrow.

MARIAN: Then why didn't you protest?

ROBIN: I wanted to let him win.

MARIAN: But you told your father—

ROBIN: That I would take the job. I know. But there was never any way I would work for the Sheriff of Nottingham. Philip gave me an easy way out. Without losing face to my father. Instead, I lost a friend and was almost arrested by your father. Just because you decided to interfere.

MARIAN: But it was unfair!

ROBIN: You heard what your father said about that.

MARIAN: I'm not like my father.

ROBIN: Well, maybe you should be! Go ahead, turn a blind eye. What's it to you? All high and mighty in your castle tower, high over the poor peasants of Nottingham. What do you care?

MARIAN: I do care. I care about justice.

ROBIN: Why should I believe you?

MARIAN: Because I want…I want to study the law. I want to be a solicitor.

ROBIN: You? A woman?

MARIAN: Why not? They've started to allow women to study the law in London.

ROBIN: Well, this isn't London. But good luck to you. *(He begins to leave.)*

MARIAN: Robin, wait. I'm sorry…for my behavior in the forest. I don't usually meet people like you.

ROBIN: Of course not. Your father hangs them.

MARIAN: True. It's hard for me to make friends.

ROBIN: You want to be…my friend?

MARIAN: I suppose.

ROBIN: Your father will never allow it. And he'll have me killed if you see me.

MARIAN: Probably. May I come tomorrow?

(Pause)

ROBIN: If you like.

MARIAN: Good.

(MARIAN kisses ROBIN's cheek. He is stunned.)

MARIAN: You better be off now—Robin of the Greenwood.

(ROBIN runs offstage.)

(Lights shift.)

Scene Four

(Night in Sherwood Forest. ROBIN walks home alone, when he encounters a small boy near a river. The boy holds a long broadstaff.)

MUCH: Come no further.

ROBIN: What do you want?

MUCH: For you to leave.

ROBIN: Stand aside, boy.

MUCH: This is our property. No one is allowed past this river.

ROBIN: No one owns this forest except King Richard.

MUCH: I'm warning you. You would be wise to turn around and forget this place. Or else you'll be thrown into the water.

ROBIN: By who? You?

MUCH: Do not doubt me, sir.

ROBIN: I smell a campfire. With meat cooking—rabbit meat. The hunting of rabbits—or any other game—is strictly forbidden in Sherwood Forest.

MUCH: Your nose fools you. It's turnip soup.

ROBIN: My father is the King's Forester.

MUCH: Prove it.

ROBIN: I don't need to. *(He takes a couple of steps forward.)*

MUCH: I tried to warn you. Now you'll be sorry.

ROBIN: Go ahead and stop me, if you think you can.

(MUCH bangs his broadstaff, and out comes JOAN, a large girl who carries her own staff.)

ROBIN: What's this? I thought I was fighting you!

MUCH: I never said that.

ROBIN: Who are you fellows?

JOAN: I'm not a fellow.

ROBIN: Then what are you?

JOAN: A female fellow.

ROBIN: I'm not going to fight a girl.

JOAN: Then don't think of me that way. Most people don't.

ROBIN: Now look. Just move aside and you won't get hurt.

JOAN: I don't plan to.

MUCH: She never gets hurt. You'd be wise to turn around.

(JOAN *throws her broadstaff at* ROBIN, *who barely catches it, the force of the throw sending him backwards.*)

(JOAN *takes* MUCH's *staff.*)

ROBIN: I've had enough of this! Prepare to get wet.

(ROBIN *tries to fight her, but is battered by the blows from* JOAN's *broadstaff. It's difficult, since he tries to direct his blows to her staff, but she aims for his body. After a few minutes of fighting, he sees his cause is lost. He throws down his broadstaff.*)

ROBIN: All right! I give up!

JOAN: Good.

(ROBIN *suddenly tries to run past* JOAN. *But she turns and trips him as he runs, knocking him into the river. A large splash is heard.*)

JOAN: This is a tricky one.

(MUCH *helps* ROBIN *out of the river.*)

MUCH: Now he's soaked. We'd better bring him back to the fire.

JOAN: What for?

MUCH: He says he's the Forester's son.

JOAN: Then we'll get in trouble. Leave him be.

MUCH: We'll get in even more trouble if he gets sick.

ROBIN: You two don't know what trouble is. Yet.

MUCH: Maybe not—but you better come with us anyway.

(JOAN *produces an apple from a pocket.*)

JOAN: At least we had a good fight. Have an apple.

ROBIN: All right.

(ROBIN *munches on the apple while they move through the forest.*)

MUCH: *(To* JOAN*)* You know, we could use someone like him.

JOAN: Hey! Good idea! *(To* ROBIN*)* You wanna join our band of outlaws?

ROBIN: Outlaws? How many of you are there?

MUCH: Well, there's us. And you, if you join us.

ROBIN: What do you call yourselves?

MUCH: What do you mean?

ROBIN: Every self-respecting band of outlaws needs a name to call themselves.

JOAN: He's right. How about…the Outlaws?

MUCH: Too obvious.

JOAN: That's your opinion. *(Turning to* ROBIN*)* I'd rather know what you think. Not Much.

ROBIN: Thanks a lot.

JOAN: For what?

ROBIN: You said "not Much".

JOAN: That's right. I'm asking you. I'm not asking Much.

ROBIN: I never said you were.

MUCH: He's confused.

JOAN: I know that, Much.

ROBIN: How much?

MUCH: Who, me?

ROBIN: What?

JOAN: You're asking Much.

ROBIN: I don't think I'm asking much.

MUCH: You don't understand. I'm Much.

ROBIN: Believe me. You're both a bit much.

JOAN: Not me. Just him.

MUCH: My name is Much! I'm Much—the miller's son.

ROBIN: Oh. That's your name? That's...really confusing.

JOAN: I'm his sister—Joan.

ROBIN: You're related?

JOAN: Mother says I'm having a growth spurt.

(The three of them move on toward a glowing fire. They encounter a campfire, with a rabbit cooking on a spit. A strange MAN *in a hooded garment tends to the rabbit, looking up at them as they enter.* ROSALIND, *a peasant woman, moves toward the newcomers with alarm.)*

ROSALIND: What have you done? You know you can't bring strangers here!

MUCH: He got too wet to leave in the woods.

ROSALIND: Who is this boy?

JOAN: He claims to be the Forester's son.

ROSALIND: Then you must take him away! At once!

(The MAN *stands.)*

MAN: No. Let him stay.

ROSALIND: Please reconsider. It isn't safe. Especially for you.

ROBIN: That's right. My father will know what to do with the likes of you.

MAN: He already does.

(The MAN *removes his hood, revealing himself to be* WILLIAM—ROBIN's *father.)*

ROBIN: Father! What are you doing here—with these people?

WILLIAM: These people have names, Robin. This is Rosalind, her son Much, and her daughter Joan.

ROSALIND: Perhaps you knew my husband. He owned the mill at the forest's edge. Until his death last month.

ROBIN: I heard about that. The mill burned down, and he was caught within its walls. A terrible accident.

JOAN: That was no accident.

ROSALIND: There was no sign of trouble until the landlord suddenly doubled the rent. With the increased taxes from Prince John, we couldn't afford that and have anything left for ourselves. So my husband gave him every sack of grain he had milled to date, and asked for more time to pay the rest.

MUCH: The mill burned down the next day.

JOAN: With father inside.

ROSALIND: I believed our own house would have been next. We took what we could and left at night. Lucky to escape with our lives.

WILLIAM: Ask them who their landlord was.

ROBIN: Who?

ROSALIND: Sir Guy of Gisbourne. As cowardly a scoundrel as ever lived.

JOAN: The next time I see him...

(JOAN *cracks a large branch in two, and throws the pieces into the fire.*)

ROBIN: But father, I don't understand. These people are breaking the law.

WILLIAM: Yes, Robin, they are. And so am I, by helping them.

ROBIN: You too?

WILLIAM: I brought them this rabbit to eat. I bring them what I can, as often as possible. And try to protect them from the consequences of Sir Guy's greed.

ROBIN: But you always tell me about the importance of obeying the law.

WILLIAM: You're still young, Robin. And it's hard to tell you that sometimes the law can be unjust and cruel. When that happens, it's a lawman's duty to allow exceptions—for the weak and vulnerable.

ROBIN: But if you can't believe in the law, what can you believe in?

WILLIAM: Your heart. For that's where the lessons of justice are learned. Are you with us?

(ROBIN *turns to the others.*)

ROBIN: Welcome to Sherwood Forest, my friends. Your secret is safe with me.

ROSALIND: Thank you both for your help and protection. What would we do without you?

WILLIAM: Just eat up. And put that fire out before anyone else notices you. Let's go, Robin. I always check on their house before I go home.

(WILLIAM *and* ROBIN *leave the area, as the others gather around the campfire.*)

(PHILIP *enters stealthily. He pauses to watch* ROBIN *and* WILLIAM *off, then raises his sword and approaches the family.*)

PHILIP: Turn around slowly, if you please. Your hands where I can see them.

(JOAN *and* MUCH *look around.*)

PHILIP: There's no place to run, I'm afraid. You're surrounded by the Sheriff's men. With orders to cut you down as soon as you try to escape. (*He throws some rope to* MUCH.) Here. Tie their hands behind them. Start with the big one.

(JOAN *starts for* PHILIP.)

JOAN: I have other plans, you rodent.

ROSALIND: Joan! Do as he says! We have no choice.

(JOAN *stops, and allows her hands to be tied by* MUCH, *as does* ROSALIND.)

(PHILIP *ties* MUCH's *hands, then forces them off at swordpoint.*)

(*Lights shift.*)

Scene Five

(ROBIN *and* WILLIAM *approach their cottage, where they are confronted by a grim group:* GUY, PHILIP *and the* SHERIFF.)

(ROSALIND *and her children are seated on the ground, their hands still tied.*)

ROSALIND: William! Run! They've come to arrest you!

(Instead of escaping, ROBIN *and* WILLIAM *come running forward.)*

WILLIAM: What's the meaning of this?

SHERIFF: Only performing my duty, Forester. Which is more than I can say for you.

GUY: These lying peasants are tenants on my property. Which they abandoned without permission. They haven't paid me rent since her husband's unfortunate mill accident. Yet they feel entitled to enter the King's Forest and kill his rabbits. My son found the evidence.

WILLIAM: They didn't kill that rabbit. It came from my own stockpile.

PHILIP: He's protecting them, your honor. And giving them food too.

GUY: Rabbit or not, there's still a matter of the rent.

ROSALIND: We have nothing left. You made sure of that when you stole my husband's grain.

GUY: He gave it to me willingly. As partial payment.

SHERIFF: It doesn't matter whether it's refusal or inability to pay. Unpaid rent receives the same punishment under the Prince's law. Imprisonment in Nottingham Dungeon.

WILLIAM: Among the rabble in that prison? Their throats will be cut within a few days.

SHERIFF: Maybe so. But that's the law.

ROBIN: It may be the law. But that doesn't always make it right.

SHERIFF: Make no mistake, boy. The law is *always* right.

WILLIAM: I'll pay their rent. What do they owe you?

GUY: Ten shillings.

WILLIAM: Fine. Will they be allowed to keep their home?

GUY: Certainly not. When they abandoned it, the property reverted to me.

WILLIAM: Which makes them homeless.

ROBIN: They can stay with us.

(During the following, GUY surreptitiously enters the cottage.)

SHERIFF: I'm afraid your own residency here is in question, Fitzooth. Harboring fugitives is not one of the duties of the King's Foresters. Even one appointed by King Richard.

WILLIAM: It was never King Richard's intention to cause starvation in his own kingdom.

SHERIFF: Unfortunately, Richard isn't around to explain his intentions. Until he returns, I serve Prince John. But the Prince has instructed me to be merciful. He will absolve your infraction for an additional payment.

WILLIAM: Will that satisfy him?

SHERIFF: Money always satisfies the Prince. I'll add it to his treasury.

WILLIAM: How much is the fine?

SHERIFF: For harboring a fugitive—ten pounds.

ROBIN: Father—you can't. That's all the money we have in the world.

WILLIAM: Robin—go inside and fetch the money. You'll find it in my room.

ROBIN: But—

WILLIAM: No argument. Now go!

(ROBIN heads for the cottage door, but is stopped by GUY, who carries a large slab of deer meat out of the house.)

GUY: One minute, your honor. I think you may want to take a look at this.

PHILIP: Venison! Where did you find this, Father?

GUY: In his stockroom.

SHERIFF: You know what this means, Fitzooth? The killing of deer in the Royal Forest is a hanging offense.

WILLIAM: I've never seen that before. Sir Guy must have placed it there. Or else his son.

SHERIFF: That's a serious accusation against one of the Sheriff's own men.

PHILIP: Your honor. Master Fitzooth has always upheld the law when it came to the hunting laws. I can't believe he would do this.

SHERIFF: Perhaps his son?

PHILIP: No. Not Robin.

SHERIFF: Then you accuse your own father of lying?

(Pause. PHILIP looks at GUY.)

PHILIP: Of course not.

SHERIFF: Well, it didn't walk in there on its own legs. William Fitzooth, you are under arrest. Take him to the dungeon, lad.

(PHILIP hesitates.)

SHERIFF: I would think the tone of my voice would discourage any hesitation.

PHILIP: Your honor, I beg you to reconsider. Master
Fitzooth has always been a loyal subject of the King.

SHERIFF: You obviously have a noble spirit, my
boy. But don't be fooled by this Forester's manner.
Apparently he has been taking advantage of his
position to kill the King's own game.

PHILIP: It can't be true.

SHERIFF: I suggest you think about your future, young
Gisbourne. It may come to an end here and now.

(PHILIP *draws his sword.*)

PHILIP: I'm sorry, Master Fitzooth. I must do my duty.

WILLIAM: Your duty, Philip? Or his?

ROBIN: We were friends a long time, Philip. It's not too
late to save that. You can refuse to take part in this.

SHERIFF: Be quiet, boy.

(WILLIAM *turns to the* SHERIFF.)

WILLIAM: That's what this was about all along, wasn't
it? You didn't want this poor family at all—you
wanted me!

SHERIFF: Don't think so highly of yourself, Fitzooth.
Besides, now that you'll all be in Nottingham Dungeon
together—maybe you can protect this mother and her
boys for a day or two.

JOAN: I'm not a boy!

(JOAN *breaks her rope, and rushes the* SHERIFF, *who turns
and threatens her with his sword. It's enough of a distraction
to allow* WILLIAM *to go to the giant oak, reach into it, and
pull out two long swords. He throws one to* ROBIN.)

WILLIAM: Robin! Catch!

(*A standoff.* WILLIAM *faces the* SHERIFF, *and* ROBIN *faces*
PHILIP—*all with swords drawn.*)

(Meanwhile, JOAN *unties* MUCH *and* ROSALIND.*)*

SHERIFF: It appears your crimes increase by the minute, Fitzooth. This is your last chance to surrender—before I kill you myself.

ROBIN: Is this a time to stand our ground, Father?

WILLIAM: It's beyond that now, Robin. Now we have no choice—but fight.

(Pause as they try to gain position, and slowly move. Finally, the SHERIFF *lunges forward, and the two pairs fight separate duels.)*

*(*JOAN *and* MUCH *try to help as much as they can, but manage to get in the way more often than not.)*

*(*ROSALIND *chases the cowardly* GUY *around the area, with whatever makeshift weapon she can wield or throw.)*

(Eventually, ROBIN *disarms* PHILIP.*)*

(And the SHERIFF *grabs* MUCH *at knifepoint, and tries to hold him as a hostage. But* MUCH *bites him, and the* SHERIFF *releases him only to find himself faced with an arrow from* ROBIN'*s bow.)*

SHERIFF: You have just signed your own death warrant, boy.

*(*WILLIAM *disarms the* SHERIFF *and guards him with the knife.)*

WILLIAM: Run, my son! Take them with you!

ROBIN: No! I will not leave you!

WILLIAM: You must! For their sake!

ROBIN: Follow me, all of you. You too, Father.

WILLIAM: I'll be right behind you.

ROSALIND: William! What are you doing?

WILLIAM: Giving you the advantage. So go!

(They back away, threatening the SHERIFF, PHILIP *and the terrified* GUY *with their swords. Finally they run off.)*

(A pause while WILLIAM *keeps the* SHERIFF *at bay with the knife.)*

SHERIFF: Are you really so foolish? Do you believe this will save your son's life?

WILLIAM: No. I don't. So I propose a bargain.

SHERIFF: What bargain?

WILLIAM: I hand myself over to you, as your prisoner. In exchange for Robin's freedom.

SHERIFF: That simple, eh?

WILLIAM: That simple.

SHERIFF: All right. I accept your bargain.

*(*WILLIAM *holds the knife to the* SHERIFF's *throat.)*

WILLIAM: You will swear to it? In the name of King Richard?

SHERIFF: I do swear it, in the name of King Richard.

*(*WILLIAM *slowly hands the knife back to the* SHERIFF. *The* SHERIFF *takes it and brings it up to* WILLIAM's *own throat.)*

SHERIFF: I should kill you now. But I need you alive. To lure your son back to Nottingham.

WILLIAM: You swore you'd let him go—in the name of the King.

SHERIFF: The King is in a foreign land, and most likely dead. You should have had me swear to Prince John.

PHILIP: But Your Honor, you did make a promise to Master Fitzooth…

SHERIFF: Fitzooth and his son will be swinging on the gallows by the end of this week. That is my true promise. I suggest you don't question it.

PHILIP: Yes sir.

(The SHERIFF *calms himself, and puts his hand on* PHILIP'*s shoulder.)*

SHERIFF: You handled yourself valiantly, Gisbourne.

*(*GUY *picks himself up from the ground, where he has been cowering.)*

GUY: Oh—thank you, Your Honor. Nothing to it.

SHERIFF: Not you. Your son. He has proven himself worthy of my highest trust. Just one last task to justify your new salary. *(He takes a lit torch down from next to the cottage door, and ceremoniously hands it to* PHILIP.*)* Burn the house down. To the ground.

WILLIAM: What kind of butcher are you?

SHERIFF: I won't have them using it for a headquarters. If your son and that lot want to behave like animals, they can live like animals—in the open forest. Well, boy? What are you waiting for?

PHILIP: Your honor—please don't ask me to do this. Rob and his father never did anything to me.

SHERIFF: But they've done quite a lot to me. Insulted me, defied me, and broke the law. Are you willing to defend the law or aren't you? Your future depends on this decision.

*(*PHILIP *takes the torch, and sets fire to some hay at the corner of the house.)*

SHERIFF: Oh, I forgot the money. Go inside and find it, will you, Sir Guy? It's in the father's room.

GUY: I'm not going in there! The house is burning!

SHERIFF: You should be used to that.

PHILIP: What does he mean by that, Father?

GUY: Nothing…I'll get it. *(He runs into the house.)*

WILLIAM: Richard will have your head. When he returns from the Crusades.

SHERIFF: It's been over four years. Do you really believe he's still alive?

WILLIAM: I do.

PHILIP: Quickly, Father! The fire is growing!

(GUY *runs out of the house juggling a hot bag of coins, which he throws to the* SHERIFF.)

PHILIP: Father—are you sure that the mill burned down by accident?

GUY: Of course I am. I remember plenty of wood shavings laying around. Very careless of the miller.

PHILIP: And this venison—

SHERIFF: Will be served tonight at the castle. You are both invited—but not you, Forester. The dungeon serves a more humble cuisine.

PHILIP: Why don't we go after Robin?

SHERIFF: Deep into Sherwood Forest? We'd only get lost—and ambushed.

WILLIAM: They'll never leave the forest.

SHERIFF: Maybe not all of them. But Robin will come for you. And when he does—I will be ready for him.

(*The* SHERIFF *motions* WILLIAM *off at sword point.* GUY *follows them with the venison.*)

(PHILIP *takes a look at the cottage, conflicted by what he has done. Then he follows them off.*)

(*Lights shift.*)

Scene Six

*(Lights up on a small area where the others—*ROBIN,
ROSALIND, MUCH *and* JOAN—*gather, watching the house
burn at a distance.)*

ROSALIND: They took him away.

ROBIN: Yes. He sacrificed himself for our sakes.

MUCH: And now your house is gone.

JOAN: And ours is still off limits.

ROBIN: Not all is lost. We're still alive.

ROSALIND: If you call this a life. We're outcasts.
Without homes, destined to spend the rest of our days
in Sherwood Forest.

ROBIN: No one knows this forest better than I do. How
to hunt, keep safe and survive.

MUCH: But we're wanted by the law.

JOAN: If only Richard were here.

MUCH: The true King.

ROSALIND: Bah. A true King would never abandon his
own citizens, to wage war in foreign lands.

ROBIN: He'll return some day. Don't lose your faith.

MUCH: So we wait for Richard?

ROBIN: No. There is no time to wait. I will not rest
until my father is freed, with his honor and position
restored.

ROSALIND: How will you do it?

ROBIN: I don't know yet. But I'll need your help.

JOAN: You have it, Robin.

MUCH: Me too.

ROSALIND: Your father saved our lives. I would do anything to repay his kindness.

(They extend their arms, piling their hands on top of each other.)

ROBIN: Excellent! In the meantime—let's all be outlaws together! To be feared and respected by all who pass this way! The kings—and queens—of Sherwood Forest!

(Lights fade out.)

END OF ACT ONE

ACT TWO

Scene One

(Lights up on an area suggesting MARIAN's *room within a tower in the* SHERIFF's *castle.)*

(The SHERIFF *is in mid-argument with his daughter,* MARIAN.*)*

MARIAN: You burned their house!

SHERIFF: To be precise, it was your young friend Philip.

MARIAN: On your instructions!

SHERIFF: Of course. The forester won't be needing it now.

MARIAN: What has happened to you, Father? Does the Prince frighten you to this extent?

SHERIFF: It's not about fear, Marian. It's about order. Sometimes you have to make an example of someone, to prevent others from getting certain ideas.

MARIAN: What ideas?

SHERIFF: That lawlessness is permissible under certain conditions. Order requires discipline. And occasionally discipline means punishment.

MARIAN: I don't think Mother would agree with you. If she were here.

(Pause)

SHERIFF: True. You're right about that. She didn't believe in discipline. Especially in the way she chose to raise you. Letting you do practically anything you wanted. As for the law, she always believed in giving people a second chance. But God didn't give her much of a chance, did he? Taking her away from us before she...before we could...

MARIAN: It wasn't God. It was smallpox. And it made you change. In such a harsh way. You became so rigid—so unforgiving. You don't need to punish the world. I miss her too.

SHERIFF: This isn't about your mother.

MARIAN: I think it is.

SHERIFF: Marian. I don't want you to think badly of me. It's just the nature of my office. If I show the slightest mercy toward lawbreakers, then the law has no meaning.

MARIAN: Well, maybe it has no meaning. And maybe you should quit your job.

SHERIFF: The Prince relies on me to do that job.

MARIAN: And pays you well.

SHERIFF: William Fitzooth has committed treasonous acts against the Prince. According to the edicts of the law, he has been removed from his post and declared an outlaw.

MARIAN: Only King Richard can do that! You have no authority over a King's Forester!

SHERIFF: I have the same authority over him that I have over you. So stop arguing with your father, or else...

MARIAN: Or else what?

(PHILIP *enters*.)

SHERIFF: I insist upon respect from my own daughter!

MARIAN: Then act respectfully! And don't think you can order me around—I'm nearly seventeen years old.

PHILIP: Your honor—should I come back later?

SHERIFF: Your timing is poor, boy. What do you want? Speak up!

PHILIP: You summoned me, sir.

SHERIFF: I did? Oh. Yes. So I did. *(He turns back to MARIAN.)* You may no longer be a girl, but you're not yet a woman. And you shall learn to obey. *(He turns to PHILIP.)* Make sure she doesn't leave the castle.

MARIAN: You can't do that!

SHERIFF: I won't have some childish infatuation over a Forester's son affect my decision. He and his father will be brought to justice.

PHILIP: Your honor—with all respect—I'm not a nursemaid.

SHERIFF: You are whatever I tell you to be. Or you will also find yourself in my dungeon. Is that clear?

PHILIP: Yes sir.

SHERIFF: She may have her freedom within the castle walls. But if she escapes—

PHILIP: That will not happen.

SHERIFF: Good. *(He turns to MARIAN.)* I will be in my study for the remainder of the night. If you care to apologize for your impertinence.

(The SHERIFF exits. MARIAN turns to PHILIP.)

MARIAN: Do you intend to follow me around all night like a dog?

PHILIP: Of course not. I only have the highest regard for you, Marian. I want you to think of me as a friend.

MARIAN: Then act as a friend. And help me rescue Robin and his father.

PHILIP: Don't be so concerned about Robin. I have much better prospects then some awkward forest boy. And I can protect you from your ogre of a father.

MARIAN: Perhaps my father would like to know how you dare to describe him to his own daughter.

PHILIP: I'm proving myself to you.

MARIAN: You're proving yourself a jackass. That awkward forest boy is ten times the man you'll ever be. And you helped trap him with stolen deer meat.

PHILIP: I knew nothing about that. And I didn't know your father would burn their house.

MARIAN: Don't lie to me—boy. You set the *fire*.

PHILIP: You're wasting your affection on Robin, you know. Because he will be hung from his neck on a rope—next to his father. But I will always be here for you.

(MARIAN *slaps* PHILIP.)

MARIAN: From this moment on, you are not allowed to speak to me. Get out of my room. But feel free to curl up and freeze outside the door—*watchdog*.

(PHILIP *exits, rubbing his face.*)

(MARIAN *calls out.*)

MARIAN: Diana! Where are you?

(DIANA *flies in and comes to* MARIAN.)

MARIAN: I have a job for you. (*She folds a note into a tiny locket on a bracelet, then goes to* DIANA *and snaps the bracelet around her neck.*) Take this to Robin. In the forest. With the green cap! Remember? Now fly!

(DIANA *flies offstage.*)

(Lights shift to a nearby area, where PHILIP *runs to the* SHERIFF.*)*

PHILIP: Your honor!

SHERIFF: What is it? Is my daughter gone already?

PHILIP: No, Your honor. But her falcon has flown toward Sherwood Forest.

(The SHERIFF *smiles.)*

SHERIFF: That was quite fast.

PHILIP: Shouldn't we try to stop it?

SHERIFF: Of course not. That bird is the device by which we will snare young Robin.

PHILIP: I don't understand.

SHERIFF: Why tramp through the woods looking for the boy, when that excellent falcon will bring him to us?

PHILIP: You think that Robin will come here—at her request.

SHERIFF: I'm counting on it.

PHILIP: But what if the falcon flies away? Or gets lost?

SHERIFF: Marian trained that bird too well. She can find a mouse on the forest floor from miles away. She will have no problem finding a green hat in the wilderness. And she will go to him. All we have to do is wait.

(Lights shift.)

Scene Two

(Later that evening, at a campsite deep in the forest.)

*(*ROSALIND *clears the area, as* ROBIN *enters with his quiver and a fresh kill of squirrels.)*

ROBIN: I had a six-point buck in my sights—but I let him go. I don't even know why.

ROSALIND: Of course you do. Your father wouldn't have approved of you breaking the Forest Laws.

ROBIN: I suppose you're right. Anyway, I managed to bag a few of these. It's not venison or boar, but they will have to do.

ROSALIND: I don't think the King will miss a few squirrels.

(JOAN *and* MUCH *enter, with a hooded* ABBOT *at their swordpoints.*)

JOAN: We found this fellow wandering near the cottage ruins.

MUCH: He claims to be a holy man—but he may be one of the Sheriff's spies.

ROBIN: We'll find out soon enough.

ROSALIND: Did you search him?

JOAN: Nothing on him but a rosary.

MUCH: And a horse. We tied it nearby.

ROSALIND: You carry no coin, Father?

ABBOT: Certainly not. I'm a man of God, and have taken a vow of poverty.

MUCH: Why would you do that?

ROBIN: Sorry, Father. It's just that some of us don't get a choice about that sort of thing.

ABBOT: Life is not about material wealth. It is about the spirit—and the goodness that comes from within.

JOAN: You're not from around here, are you?

ABBOT: Not for several years. I was in Cyprus, then Jerusalem. Then Austria.

ROBIN: Jerusalem? You were on the Crusades? Did you see King Richard?

ABBOT: I did indeed. I've spent many months making my way back to King Richard's castle.

JOAN: With no protection but a rosary?

ABBOT: Only the generosity of strangers—such as yourselves.

ROSALIND: Never mind that. Tell us about the King! Is he alive?

ABBOT: He most certainly is.

(The outlaws exclaim in delight.)

ROBIN: This is fantastic news! When is he coming home?

ABBOT: Not for a while, I'm afraid. King Richard has been taken prisoner in Austria.

ROBIN: Imprisoned!

ABBOT: That's why I was sent here by Duke Leopold— to negotiate the terms of his release with Richard's brother, the Prince.

ROSALIND: Then we're truly lost.

ABBOT: I beg your pardon? I'll have you know I'm quite renowned for my bargaining skills.

ROBIN: It's not about you, Father. You don't know Prince John. He's given special powers to the Sheriff of Nottingham, to tax the peasantry. John would rather keep the King in prison.

ABBOT: I see. That is unfortunate.

ROSALIND: It's the King's own fault. He should have stayed home, to watch over his own citizens. Instead of wasting his time with foreign adventures.

ABBOT: Perhaps. I'm not very familiar with political matters.

(They gather around the campfire, as ROSALIND *begins to skin the squirrel.)*

ROSALIND: Hmm. It must be nice to have one's head in the clouds. You have a lot to learn.

ABBOT: Much.

MUCH: Yes, Father?

ABBOT: Yes what?

MUCH: What do you want?

ABBOT: What do you mean?

MUCH: You said Much!

ABBOT: I don't remember saying much of anything.

ROBIN: This could go on forever. His name is Much.

ABBOT: Much what?

ROBIN: I'll try it backwards. Much—is his name.

ABBOT: Oh! That's…really confusing. *(He turns to* JOAN.) What about you? You don't say much, do you?

JOAN: Why should I? He's right here.

ABBOT: Of course.

JOAN: I'm Joan.

ABBOT: John, eh? That's a nice sturdy name for a big strapping fellow like you.

JOAN: I'm not a big strapping fellow.

ABBOT: Of course not. You're just a little slip of a thing, aren't you? Little John!

JOAN: My name is—

ABBOT: Little John, yes. I'll remember that. And you, sir? I take it you're the leader of this threadbare band of thieves?

ROBIN: Robin Fitzooth. Although we haven't actually succeeded in robbing anyone yet.

ABBOT: Fitzooth? I believe I remember a Fitzooth—
one of the King's Foresters, I believe. Appointed by
Richard?

ROBIN: That's my father!

ABBOT: Excellent! I was hoping to find his cottage this
morning, and ask to spend the night. But all I found
was the ruins of a recent fire.

ROBIN: A sad tale, I'm afraid. My father was removed
from his post by the Sheriff. And his home burnt to the
ground.

ABBOT: What? This is harsh news. Where is he now?

ROBIN: In Nottingham dungeon. He tried to protect this
family from the wrath of Sir Guy of Gisbourne. In turn,
they accused him of killing the King's deer.

ABBOT: A grave charge, indeed. Was he guilty of
poaching?

ROBIN: Never. My father devoted his life to protecting
Sherwood Forest, in service to good King Richard.
Now he awaits a hangman's noose.

ABBOT: What do you plan to do?

ROBIN: Attempt to free my father from Nottingham.

ABBOT: How?

ROBIN: I don't know.

ABBOT: But if you fail, you will join him on the gallows.
You're much too young to die.

ROBIN: Then I must make sure his rescue succeeds.
Enough about our troubles. Please, rest and have your
fill of the King's squirrels.

ABBOT: You realize that even if your father is innocent,
you're now breaking the law in this forest.

ROBIN: Yes, Father. And so are you, when you have a
bite of these measly squirrels.

(The festivities are interrupted by the sudden appearance of DIANA *who flies at* ROBIN's *head, startling him and the others.)*

ABBOT: My heavens!

ROSALIND: What is it?

JOAN: A hawk!

MUCH: I'll get it!

*(*MUCH *grabs an arrow from* ROBIN's *quiver. He places it in the bow and dangerously tries to aim it at* ROBIN's *head.)*

ROSALIND: Stop that! *(She grabs the bow away from* MUCH.*)* What do you think you're doing?

MUCH: I'm just trying to shoot the hawk.

ROBIN: It's not a hawk, it's Marian's falcon! Nobody hurt it!

ABBOT: She must be here for a reason. Here. *(He throws a cloth to* ROBIN.*)* See if she'll light on your arm. Wrap this around it.

*(*ROBIN *wraps the cloth around his arm, then extends it.* DIANA *gently lands on the cloth, looking at* ROBIN.*)*

ROBIN: I can still feel those claws.

JOAN: There's something around its neck.

ROSALIND: It's a bracelet!

ROBIN: Let me see it.

*(*ROBIN *tries to remove the bracelet from* DIANA's *neck, but it tries to bite him.)*

ROBIN: Diana—listen to me. If you don't calm down, I will put you on a rotisserie and we will have you for supper.

*(*DIANA *settles down, and allows* ROBIN *to remove the bracelet.)*

ROBIN: There's a locket here. *(He opens the locket and removes the note.)* And a note.

MUCH: What's it say?

ROBIN: It's from Marian. She says…she saw my father.

ROSALIND: Is that all?

ROBIN: And he is well. *(He addresses* DIANA.) Fly back to Marian. Fly!

*(*DIANA *takes off from his arm, circles the encampment, then flies off in the moonlight.)*

ROSALIND: It's getting late. Let's to bed. We can be up with the rabbits and catch a few for tomorrow's dinner. *(She hands the* ABBOT *a quilt.)* Here, Father. This should keep you warm tonight.

ABBOT: You are all very kind.

*(*ROSALIND *puts out the fire. Everyone beds down for the night.)*

(Time passes as the night gets dark.)

(The stag returns and stands over the ABBOT *while he sleeps, then moves off.)*

*(*ROBIN *stirs and goes to the* ABBOT, *who lies under the quilt.)*

ROBIN: Father.

(The ABBOT *comes to, startled. He grabs* ROBIN *by the scruff of his neck, then lets him go upon recognition.)*

ABBOT: That's a good way to get yourself killed, my young friend.

ROBIN: Good reflexes for a priest.

ABBOT: God's enemies are all around. One must be vigilant. What do you want?

ROBIN: Lower your voice, please. I'd like to borrow your horse.

ABBOT: I told you—I must make my way tomorrow to King Richard's castle.

ROBIN: Where the knights may slit your throat. I wouldn't be in such a hurry if I were you.

ABBOT: What do you want my horse for?

(ROBIN *shows the* ABBOT *the note from* MARIAN*'s locket.*)

ABBOT: Ah. I knew there must be more to this note.

ROBIN: She has a plan to rescue my father from Nottingham Dungeon.

ABBOT: This girl you speak of... Is she not the Sheriff's daughter?

ROBIN: That's right.

ABBOT: And yet you trust her?

ROBIN: I think I do. I must. I have no choice.

(*The* ABBOT *begins to rise.*)

ROBIN: Where are you going?

ABBOT: I'll take you there.

ROBIN: No, Father. I must go alone for her plan to work.

ABBOT: If the Sheriff catches you, it will be you *and* your father hanging on the gallows.

ROBIN: I have to take that chance. But you can help me further if you're willing.

ABBOT: Just name it. What can I do?

ROBIN: You can give me your monk's robes.

(*The* ABBOT *stares at* ROBIN, *then begins to remove his garments as lights shift.*)

Scene Three

(Lights up later that night on Nottingham dungeon, a dark and dank cell. Moonlight comes through a small window, illuminating the figure of WILLIAM, *sitting against a wall. He looks up as the cell door opens.)*

(A CELLKEEPER *enters, followed by* MARIAN, *carrying a small basket of fruit.)*

MARIAN: You may leave me alone with the Forester.

(The CELLKEEPER *hesitates.)*

MARIAN: Should I tell my Father of your rudeness? He wants to make sure this prisoner doesn't contract scurvy before his public execution. *(She hands him a bottle of wine.)* Perhaps you can quench your thirst while you wait.

(Eyeing MARIAN *and* WILLIAM *suspiciously, the* CELLKEEPER *takes the bottle, holds up five fingers, and exits.)*

MARIAN: We only have five minutes. You must listen to me.

WILLIAM: I don't need charity from the Sheriff's daughter. Give your fruit to some other resident of Nottingham dungeon, who might be forced to live a little longer than me.

MARIAN: I am not like my father, Master Fitzooth.

WILLIAM: No?

MARIAN: He has done you and Robin a grave injustice. It is my intention to free you from this dungeon.

WILLIAM: Is that so? I don't suppose you have a key hidden under those oranges?

MARIAN: No. I thought the Cellkeeper would search me thoroughly.

WILLIAM: I'm surprised he didn't.

MARIAN: But I do have access to all the keys of this castle. The key to this cell will be brought to me shortly.

WILLIAM: What are you talking about?

MARIAN: Take a look out the window. Beyond the castle walls.

(WILLIAM *looks at* MARIAN *strangely, then pulls a bench below the tiny window. Standing on the bench, he looks below.*)

WILLIAM: What am I supposed to look at? I don't see anything below but a monk. Holding something on his arm.

MARIAN: That's my falcon. Wave at the monk.

(WILLIAM *hesitates, then waves below.*)

WILLIAM: My heavens. It's Robin!

MARIAN: Here to free you. With my help.

(WILLIAM *quickly comes down off the bench and goes to her, whispering.*)

WILLIAM: Are you mad, girl? Your father will not hesitate to punish you as well, if you're discovered.

MARIAN: I'm aware of that.

WILLIAM: Don't sacrifice your safety for my sake, Marian. You have a secure future here in this castle. Under your father's protection.

MARIAN: But no freedom. And a life without that—as luxurious as the prison may be—is no life at all. Surely you understand that.

WILLIAM: But still—he is your father.

MARIAN: Not any more. Today, I am my own woman. And I see my father for who he is. A criminal, who terrorizes and punishes the poor people of Nottinghamshire.

WILLIAM: Then you will be an outlaw in the forest.
Along with us.

MARIAN: I cannot ask for better company. *(She climbs up on the bench and waves a red ribbon out the window.)*

(MARIAN waits until DIANA lands on the ledge of the barred window.)

MARIAN: Good girl, Diana! *(She takes a string from around the bird's head—it holds a large key.)* Fly to Robin!

(DIANA takes off and out of sight.)

(MARIAN hands the key to WILLIAM.

WILLIAM: Am I to simply walk out of here?

MARIAN: I bribed the cellkeeper with some wine. It contains a strong powder that will put him to sleep within the hour.

WILLIAM: Tell my son I will meet him at our usual rendezvous, in the forest.

(The CELLKEEPER opens the cell door, a bit awkwardly since he is holding the wine bottle in his other hand, and is starting to feel its effects.)

(WILLIAM quickly hides the key.)

(The CELLKEEPER gestures for MARIAN to leave.)

MARIAN: May God be with you, Master Fitzooth. *(She exits.)*

(The CELLKEEPER looks at WILLIAM with menace, and closes the cell door. Then he quickly passes out, outside the door. WILLIAM uses his key to open the door. He steps over the CELLKEEPER, who stirs for an instant. WILLIAM freezes. The CELLKEEPER quickly passes out again. WILLIAM exits.)

(Lights shift.)

Scene Four

(The following day, as the sun shines through the trees in the midst of Sherwood Forest, where ROBIN *walks with* MARIAN.*)*

ROBIN: My father was right, you know. This is no life for the likes of you. You should go back to the castle before it's too late.

MARIAN: I believe I'm old enough to make decisions regarding my own future.

ROBIN: Then why don't you show a little sense?

MARIAN: Perhaps you simply don't care for my company.

ROBIN: Naw. You're all right. It's just that...you being a lady and all...this just ain't the place for you.

MARIAN: Well, I like the forest. It's very clean...and quiet. When you're not jabbering at me, that is.

*(*ROBIN *snorts in protest—which is answered by a louder snort, nearby. They turn toward the noise, startled to see a bear.* ROBIN *claps his hands.)*

ROBIN: Go off with you! Go now!

(The bear moves off.)

MARIAN: Was that a bear?

ROBIN: She won't be back, don't worry. They're generally pretty shy creatures.

MARIAN: Why didn't you kill it with an arrow?

ROBIN: She's not an "it". And what if I missed? Or just wounded her? We'd be done for.

MARIAN: But you never miss. I've seen you shoot.

ROBIN: Better that she nurses her cubs, and allows them to grow.

MARIAN: You have your own Forest Laws, don't you?

ROBIN: Maybe. I do think the forest and its animals should be protected. So that it can provide meat, timber and hides. But for the truly needy—not the rich. They just see the forest as their playground.

MARIAN: Is it so wrong to play in the forest?

ROBIN: Not at all—as long as you leave it the way you found it.

MARIAN: You're a curious boy. You seem to care more for trees and animals then you do for people.

ROBIN: Why not? People lie, steal, and cause pain. The forest only gives beauty and protects the animals.

MARIAN: But it's so quiet here.

ROBIN: You said you liked the quiet.

MARIAN: At first. I'm beginning to miss the sounds of Nottingham.

ROBIN: What, the shouts of street peddlers and wagon wheels on cobblestones? I prefer these sounds.

MARIAN: What sounds? I don't hear anything.

ROBIN: Then be still and listen.

(MARIAN and ROBIN *stop and listen to the forest in the moonlight.*)

(*Pause. Sound of the wind blowing through the leaves.*)

ROBIN: Hear that? The sound of treetops bending in the wind.

(*Pause. Sound of a faraway, high-pitched shriek.*)

ROBIN: An owl seeing its prey.

(*Pause. Sound of a small animal running through the brush.*)

ROBIN: The rustling of a fox. Or maybe a bobcat.

(ROBIN *walks on.* MARIAN *is affected.*)

MARIAN: You have shown much bravery, Robin
Fitzooth. I have decided you are worthy of my favor.

ROBIN: What does that mean?

MARIAN: I shall allow you to marry me.

(ROBIN *stops.*)

ROBIN: Allow me to what?

MARIAN: You may consider yourself fortunate to have
won my heart. I've had knights offer themselves.
Dukes. Men of fortune and influence. But I have
decided to accept the love of a poor simple boy without
any prospects. Such is the fate of the heart, I suppose.

ROBIN: Now wait a minute. I haven't offered *anything*.
In the first place, I'm only sixteen. In the second place,
no one has to allow me to do anything. And in the
third place, did you say *marry you*?

MARIAN: That's right.

ROBIN: I'm not ready for that!

MARIAN: Quite right. We have not have the proper
period of courtship. You may, however, kiss my hand.

ROBIN: No thanks!

MARIAN: Very well. We'll save that for later as well. In
the meantime, you will court me in the proper fashion,
here in Sherwood Forest.

ROBIN: MARIAN, with all due respect—are you crazy?
There's nothing in the forest for you, and no way for a
pampered girl like you to survive. We have been living
on rabbit and squirrel meat. Back at the castle you have
warmth, food, and security.

MARIAN: But you left something out. Something
important.

ROBIN: I can't imagine what. (*He begins to move on, then
freezes.*) Shh. Listen.

(A muffled noise in the distance.)

MARIAN: Is it the bear again?

ROBIN: No. It's human.

(MARIAN and ROBIN run on, only to face WILLIAM, his hands bound and his mouth muzzled with a cloth. He frantically shakes his head no, trying to warn ROBIN through his gag.)

ROBIN: Father!

(ROBIN runs to WILLIAM and unties his gag.)

WILLIAM: You foolish boy. Now they have you too.

(The SHERIFF enters through the trees with PHILIP, swords drawn.)

SHERIFF: Allow me to add my thanks, Marian. You played your part marvelously.

ROBIN: What's this? A betrayal?

MARIAN: No! I swear, Robin! I had nothing to do with this!

(ROBIN pulls his bow and reaches for an arrow from his quiver.)

SHERIFF: Not the brightest idea, boy. My men outnumber you and your little group five to one. Philip, take his weapon.

ROBIN: You again. Is there no treachery that you will not embrace, if it means advancing your own fortunes?

(PHILIP takes his bow.)

PHILIP: This is your doing, Rob. Not mine. We simply followed your father.

MARIAN: You allowed me to leave the castle—and William too—on purpose?

PHILIP: As soon as you released your falcon, I knew Robin would come. But I was surprised that he didn't enter the castle.

WILLIAM: You watched me escape.

SHERIFF: We did indeed. And here we are.

ROBIN: *(To* PHILIP*)* I used to call you my friend.

SHERIFF: Friendships change. Usually replaced by ambition. And this boy is one of the most ambitious I've had the privilege to encounter.

MARIAN: Father, I insist you set these people free.

SHERIFF: I have been too tolerant with you, daughter. Your loyalty has been warped by your feelings for these peasants. Compassion is one thing, but disobedience is another. Perhaps the sight of Robin and his father swinging from a rope will be enough for you to respect my authority.

MARIAN: I can never respect a man who terrorizes and abuses those who are weaker than him. You're a coward.

SHERIFF: I warn you, Marian! Do not test my anger!

MARIAN: I'm only glad my mother didn't live long enough to see this. She would have been ashamed of you.

(Pause)

SHERIFF: Gentlemen. The dungeon awaits. With no more visits from my daughter, or anyone else. You'll be hanged tomorrow.

*(*SHERIFF *escorts them off, leaving* PHILIP *alone with* MARIAN.*)*

PHILIP: Marian.

MARIAN: What do you want, you jackal?

PHILIP: Is there nothing I can do? To make you think more kindly upon me? For I would truly treasure a change in your attitude toward me.

MARIAN: You seek forgiveness from me?

PHILIP: I do.

MARIAN: Then there is only one thing you can do. Save Robin and his father from execution.

PHILIP: How can I do that? I have sworn my allegiance to the Sheriff.

MARIAN: Then you've made your choice, haven't you? As far as I am concerned, you are dead to me. I only wish you could take their place on the gallows. *(She exits the opposite way.)*

(PHILIP follows the prisoners, dejected.)

(Lights shift.)

Scene Five

(That night in Nottingham dungeon, now occupied by both ROBIN and his father.)

ROBIN: I'm so sorry, Father. This is all my fault.

WILLIAM: Don't blame yourself, son. You're still an innocent boy, and haven't developed the seasoned cunning of that ruthless Sheriff.

ROBIN: Innocent? You mean naïve. To trust a Sheriff's daughter.

WILLIAM: Don't blame her either, Robin. I can tell she only meant to help. The two of you are equally innocent in this. She's a courageous girl. I only wish you would have had more opportunity to discover that yourself.

ROBIN: You mean…before you and I…

WILLIAM: Hush now. It profits neither of us to discuss our fates.

ROBIN: Is there no one left to help us now?

WILLIAM: I'm afraid not, son. No talented falcons, no spirited girls, no nobles, no...

ROBIN: No kings—returning from battle.

WILLIAM: Perhaps I was deluded by that hope as well.

ROBIN: At least...when they take our bodies down from the gallows...

WILLIAM: Please. No more.

ROBIN: At least you and I will still be together.

(WILLIAM *hesitates, then holds* ROBIN *tightly to his chest.*)

WILLIAM: That we will, son. Our souls may leave our mortal flesh, but you and I will be together in eternity. I'm sure of it.

(*The sun begins to rise.*)

(*A hooded* EXECUTIONER *appears, to escort* ROBIN *and* WILLIAM *to the gallows.*)

Scene Six

(*Morning in the castle courtyard*)

(*The* EXECUTIONER *brings in* ROBIN *and* WILLIAM. *He drops two nooses from above, testing the scaffold.*)

(PHILIP *enters, followed by the* SHERIFF.)

SHERIFF: A lovely morning for an execution, don't you think? I've been looking forward to this day so long, I'm almost a bit sad to see it arrive. Allow me a moment. (*Pause, as he closes his eyes.*) Done. Executioner, hood them.

(The EXECUTIONER *begins to tie* ROBIN's *and* WILLIAM's
*hands and place cloth hoods over their heads. Then he places
the nooses over their heads and tightens them.)*

WILLIAM: The people will remember this day.

SHERIFF: They certainly will. I count on this day to
instill fear and obedience into these people. There will
be no more grousing about taxes and Forest Laws, I
can promise you that. *(He checks on the* EXECUTIONER's
progress. He addresses the crowd.) William and Robin
Fitzooth, you are charged with thievery, treason and
disobedience of the Forest Laws. Worst of all, you
have resisted arrest and threatened the Sheriff and
his appointed officers with bodily harm. Under the
authority given to me by Prince John, in the name of
the County of Nottinghamshire, I herby condemn you
to death by hanging.

*(*PHILIP *shouts.)*

PHILIP: Now, Marian!

*(*MARIAN *enters with* DIANA.*)*

MARIAN: Diana! Fly!

*(*DIANA *enters and goes after the* EXECUTIONER, *chasing
him offstage.)*

SHERIFF: Will someone kill that damned bird? Once and
for all!

WILLIAM: Robin? What's going on?

ROBIN: Apparently we're being rescued?

*(*PHILIP *unsheaths his sword.)*

PHILIP: I am not a murderer. These people do not
deserve to die.

SHERIFF: You sentimental idiot. What sort of plan is
this? You, a girl and a trained falcon? Against my best
archers? Look around. They aim at you as we speak.

PHILIP: And we aim at them.

(JOAN, MUCH *and* ROSALIND *run on, aiming bows and arrows at the unseen men.*)

SHERIFF: The Miller's family? Is that all? (*He shouts out.*) Remove this rabble! And as for you—

(*The* SHERIFF *draws his sword. He prepares to fight* PHILIP.)

MARIAN: Robin! Show me your hands!

(ROBIN *sticks his hands out, and* MARIAN *shoots an arrow through the rope tying his hands.*)

(*The* SHERIFF *lunges at* PHILIP, *and their broadswords clash. This is a fierce fight, but the* SHERIFF *clearly has the advantage.* PHILIP *must block more blows than he can possibly attempt to land.*)

(*Meanwhile,* ROBIN *unsuccessfully tries to free* WILLIAM.)

(*Finally, the* SHERIFF *knocks away* PHILIP'*s sword.*)

SHERIFF: Let this be a lesson to all of you. Never send a boy to do a man's job.

(SHERIFF *prepares to strike* PHILIP, *but* ROBIN *picks up* PHILIP'*s sword and jumps between them.*)

ROBIN: Perhaps this boy can finish the job.

(*The second half of the swordfight ensues, with* ROBIN *showing skill, speed and strength. Eventually,* ROBIN *wounds the* SHERIFF *in the arm. He drops his sword.*)

SHERIFF: You appear to have won the day, young Robin. (*Suddenly, he pulls a knife from his waist.*) But appearances can be deceiving! There's more than one way to execute a prisoner. Even if I have to do it myself. (*He begins to throw the knife at* WILLIAM, *who is still bound.*)

(*Meanwhile,* MARIAN *is prepared for this, bow drawn and arrow aimed.*)

MARIAN: Don't do it, Father!

(The SHERIFF *looks at* MARIAN *and hesitates.)*

MARIAN: I'm warning you.

SHERIFF: You would not kill your own father.

*(*MARIAN *lowers her aim a bit and looks at the* SHERIFF.*)*

MARIAN: No. I would not.

SHERIFF: That's my girl. *(He begins to throw the knife.)*

(But MARIAN *shoots an arrow, knocking the knife from his hand.)*

ROBIN: Great shot, Marian!

(A blast of horn is heard, along with the sound of horses galloping near.)

MARIAN: The King's knights!

*(*MUCH *manages to free* WILLIAM, *while* PHILIP *keeps guard over the* SHERIFF.*)*

*(*KING RICHARD *walks into the scene, now wearing his royal regalia rather than the robes of the* ABBOT.*)*

KING RICHARD: I trust I'm not too late... Ah, William. I see you and your son are still among us. Good.

WILLIAM: Your highness!

*(*WILLIAM *falls to his knees, as does everyone else [possibly even the* SHERIFF*]. Only* MUCH *remains standing.)*

MUCH: What's wrong with everybody? It's just the monk from the woods.

JOAN: Not any more!

KING RICHARD: Maybe this will help the boy. I don't like to wear this when I'm riding. *(He produces a crown, which he places on his head.)*

*(*MUCH *throws himself on the ground, prostrate with fear.)*

MUCH: Your majesty!

KING RICHARD: Rise, Much. And you too, Little John.

JOAN: I'm not—

KING RICHARD: You're not what?

JOAN: Nothing, your highness. Whatever you say is fine with me.

KING RICHARD: And you, William Fitzooth. Your alleged crimes are hereby pardoned, by order of the King. And yours, too, Sir Robin.

ROBIN: Sir Robin, my lord?

KING RICHARD: Come here, my young friend. And kneel.

(ROBIN *comes to* KING RICHARD *and kneels before him.*)

(KING RICHARD *notices a discarded hood from the scaffold, and picks it up. He places a sword on* ROBIN's *shoulder.*)

KING RICHARD: In honor of your service to the grateful citizens of Nottingham, I hereby declare you an honorary King's Knight. All hail Sir Robin— (*Handing him the hood*) Hood.

ALL: Hail, Sir Robin!

(*The* SHERIFF *approaches* KING RICHARD.)

SHERIFF: Your worship, a moment if you please. If only I had known you were back—I would have consulted with you first. I'm in serious need of spiritual training.

KING RICHARD: Which you will receive on a daily basis—in Nottingham dungeon. Until your trial.

SHERIFF: Thank you, Sire.

MARIAN: Don't worry, Father. I'll visit you every day.

SHERIFF: That's a mixed blessing, I'm sure.

(GUY *enters, a bit disheveled.*)

GUY: What is the meaning of this? Why was I brought here by the King's knights?

KING RICHARD: On my instructions, Sir Guy.

GUY: *Your* instructions? Who do you think you...you... *(Recognizing him)* You? You're supposed to be dead!

KING RICHARD: A helpful rumor. I brought you here regarding certain accusations against your son, Philip.

GUY: What accusations?

KING RICHARD: The miller's family has told me all about their harassment at the hands of this boy.

ROBIN: Your majesty. Be merciful. Philip did it out of fear.

KING RICHARD: And hope of advancement, I understand.

ROBIN: But he disobeyed the Sheriff. At his own peril.

KING RICHARD: I'm glad to hear it. But I don't know. His behavior has been erratic, to say the least.

GUY: These course pursuits are obviously beneath Philip. A nobleman is above the law.

KING RICHARD: Interesting point. Would you agree, Philip?

PHILIP: No, your highness. The law applies to all equally.

KING RICHARD: Very well. If that's what you believe ...then you might be interested in becoming our new Sheriff.

PHILIP: Your majesty—I am not worthy.

KING RICHARD: I agree. And you are quite young. But perhaps you can still prove yourself a capable lawman.

PHILIP: Then let me begin now.

(PHILIP *approaches* ROSALIND, *and pulls her by the arm to center stage.*)

ROBIN: Philip! What are you doing?

PHILIP: Enforcing the King's law.

ROSALIND: Unhand me this instant!

GUY: Don't listen to her, Philip. She's a vagrant and a trespasser! Do your duty!

PHILIP: That I shall do, Father. *(He turns to his father as he lets go of* ROSALIND's *arm.)* Sir Guy of Gisbourne, you are under arrest for the murder of this woman's husband, the miller.

GUY: Philip! What are you doing?

SHERIFF: You would arrest your own father, boy?

PHILIP: That I would. In the name of the law.

SHERIFF: Impressive.

KING RICHARD: Do you have any evidence to support this claim, young man?

PHILIP: Evidence?

KING RICHARD: Yes. Any proof? Any witnesses who may testify as to the truth of this charge?

SHERIFF: Excuse me, Your Highness.

(Everyone turns to the SHERIFF.*)*

SHERIFF: I may have something to offer you in that regard.

KING RICHARD: Then let's hear it!

MARIAN: Just a minute, father. *(Turning to the* KING RICHARD*)* My father refuses to speak further without a reconsideration of his sentence.

KING RICHARD: Young lady. Do you mean to bargain with your King?

MARIAN: No more than the barristers in your Royal Court bargain for your subjects' lives.

KING RICHARD: I see. You might make a good barrister yourself, my dear. If only you were a man.

MARIAN: I beg to differ, Your Highness. I believe my gender would give me a distinct advantage in the legal profession.

KING RICHARD: That it might. Very well, Sheriff. We will discuss the terms of your imprisonment within the week. Depending on the strength of your information.

SHERIFF: Thank you, Your Highness. And thanks to you, Marian. *(He kisses her head in relief.)*

GUY: How sweet. What is going on here? This is completely unfair! You're commuting his sentence? He hanged dozens of unfortunate citizens.

KING RICHARD: There is a difference between being over-zealous in one's official duties—and cold-blooded murder.

GUY: But I didn't even know the miller was inside when— *(He realizes his error and covers his mouth.)*

ROBIN: When *what*, exactly?

GUY: I don't feel so well.

KING RICHARD: We can remedy that. One way or another. *(He addresses the crowd.)* Citizens of Nottinghamshire. Prince John has fled, and my knights have returned to me. I have neglected my kingdom, but I intend to stay. No more— *(Turning toward ROSALIND)* —foreign adventures.

(ROSALIND bows her head in embarrassment.)

KING RICHARD: William Fitzooth, you shall have a new cottage in Sherwood. If you will agree to return to your post as the King's Chief Forester. There's no one I would trust more than you to preserve and protect my forest.

WILLIAM: Of course, Sire.

KING RICHARD: And fair Rosalind, you and your children may return to your home forthwith. As its new owner—paid in full.

ROSALIND: With much gratitude, Your Highness. Maybe this Forester can stay with us—until his own cottage is rebuilt.

KING RICHARD: Of course.

WILLIAM: That's too much to ask of you, Rosalind. Why would you want to—

(ROSALIND *takes* WILLIAM's *hand in hers.*)

WILLIAM: Oh.

(ROSALIND *and* WILLIAM *walk off together.*)

KING RICHARD: Little John—and Much, of course. Would you bring the previous Sheriff and Sir Guy to my men? They'll be happy to escort them to their new lodgings.

JOAN: Glad to. May I break a few bones on the way?

KING RICHARD: Not right now.

MUCH: Showoff.

SHERIFF: Marion. Your mother…

MARIAN: Yes, Father?

SHERIFF: I think she would have been very proud of you today.

(GUY *turns to* PHILIP.)

GUY: As for you…you have betrayed me, boy. I hereby disinherit you. Do you hear me? You are no son of mine!

SHERIFF: Come, Sir Guy. Let's discuss old times during my brief incarceration.

(JOAN *and* MUCH *take* GUY *and the* SHERIFF *off.*)

KING RICHARD: What has been happening in my absence? It seems it's now up to the children to speak up and correct the mistakes of their elders. What do we call that?

(Pause)

ROBIN: Progress?

(KING RICHARD nods at ROBIN quizzically. He exits after the others.)

(PHILIP and ROBIN approach MARIAN.)

PHILIP: Um…about those arrows?

ROBIN: Yes, where did you learn—

MARIAN: You boys aren't the only archers in Nottingham, you know.

PHILIP: Perhaps we should have our own competition.

ROBIN: Perhaps we already do.

PHILIP: That's up to the lady. Well, Marion?

MARIAN: Yes?

PHILIP: You told me that you would reconsider your feelings for me. By rescuing this boy and his father. I believe I have met my end of the bargain.

MARIAN: I'm sorry, Philip. You misunderstood.

PHILIP: I understood very clearly. We had a deal.

MARIAN: A *deal*? I do not make deals. At least as far as my own affections are concerned. But if I misled you in any way, I apologize.

PHILIP: I'm sorry…for my confusion.

MARIAN: You are forgiven, Philip. Don't give it another thought. I do appreciate everything you've done.

ROBIN: As do I. With all my heart.

MARIAN: And congratulations on your new appointment. I'm sure you will make an excellent sheriff.

(She kisses him on the cheek.)

ROBIN: I hope to see you again, my friend.

PHILIP: You will, I promise.

(MARIAN and ROBIN walk away together.)

PHILIP: *(With bitterness)* Sir Robin *Hood.*

(PHILIP exits, following the others to Nottingham dungeon.)

MARIAN: I have many plans for this forest.

ROBIN: I'm sure you would prefer to live in Nottingham. Much safer for a lady.

MARIAN: Safer, but not as interesting. Besides, I think I can find someone around here to protect me.

ROBIN: After today, I don't believe you need much protection at all.

MARIAN: True. Very true. Are you ready?

ROBIN: For what?

MARIAN: Our courtship may begin now.

ROBIN: I don't think you've been listening. There is no courtship.

MARIAN: First rule of courtship. When beginning a courtship, it is considered impolite to deny it.

ROBIN: What? That makes no sense!

MARIAN: Second rule. Always remove your hat in the presence of a lady.

ROBIN: I will do no such thing.

MARIAN: Diana!

(DIANA flies on, grabs the hat from ROBIN's head, and flies offstage.)

ROBIN: Hey! Come back here! *(He runs off after the falcon.)*

MARIAN: Third rule. Never leave a lady unattended.

(ROBIN saunters back, hatless.)

ROBIN: Is there a fourth rule?

MARIAN: There are dozens of rules. But three is enough for today.

ROBIN: Good. I'm tired of rules.

(ROBIN takes MARIAN in his arms, and kisses her. She pushes him away, startled. They stare at each other.)

MARIAN: So am I.

(MARIAN grabs ROBIN and pulls his mouth to hers.)

END OF PLAY

www.ingramcontent.com/pod-product-compliance
Lightning Source LLC
Chambersburg PA
CBHW052212090426
42741CB00010B/2513